Online PRIVACY

By Julie Schwab Marzolf

Gareth Stevens
Publishing

Please visit our website, www.garethstevens.com. For a free color catalog of all our high-quality books, call toll free 1-800-542-2595 or fax 1-877-542-2596.

Library of Congress Cataloging-in-Publication Data

Marzolf, Julie Schwab.
 Online privacy / Julie Schwab Marzolf.
     p. cm. — (Cyberspace survival guide)
 Includes index.
 ISBN 978-1-4339-7225-6 (pbk.)
 ISBN 978-1-4339-7226-3 (6-pack)
 ISBN 978-1-4339-7224-9 (library binding)
 1. Internet—Safety measures. 2. Computer security. 3. Data protection. I. Title.
 TK5105.875.I57M36773 2013
 005.8—dc23
                                    2012012221

First Edition

Published in 2013 by
Gareth Stevens Publishing
111 East 14th Street, Suite 349
New York, NY 10003

Copyright © 2013 Gareth Stevens Publishing

Designer: Katelyn E. Reynolds
Editor: Therese M. Shea

Photo credits: Cover, p. 1 Chris Collins/Shutterstock.com; cover, pp. 1, 3–24 (background) Gala/ Shutterstock.com; cover, pp. 1, 3–24 (grunge banner; cursor graphics; search box graphic) Amgun/ Shutterstock.com; p. 5 Michael Shay/Taxi/Getty Images; p. 7 Hemera/Thinkstock.com; p. 8 Monkey Business/Thinkstock.com; p. 9 © iStockphoto.com/Stratol; p. 10 Comstock/Thinkstock.com; p. 11 Vanessa Davies/Dorling Kindersley/Getty Images; pp. 12, 18, 27 iStockphoto/Thinkstock.com; p. 14 rodania/Shutterstock.com; p. 15 © iStockphoto.com/vm; p. 17 PaulPaladin/Shutterstock.com; p. 19 © iStockphoto.com/spxChrome; p. 21 © iStockphoto.com/samxmeg; p. 23 Antonio M. Rosario/ Brand X Pictures/Getty Images; p. 25 Michael Krasowitz/Photographer's Choice/Getty Images; p. 28 Hasloo Group Production Studio/Shutterstock.com.

Printed in the United States of America

CPSIA compliance information: Batch #CS12GS: For further information contact Gareth Stevens, New York, New York at 1-800-542-2595.

CONTENTS

Q Words in the glossary appear in **bold** type the first time they are used in the text.

Online Privacy: WHAT IS IT?

Have you ever put a "Keep Out!" sign on your bedroom door? You might have been trying to keep your brother, sister, or even parents out of your room. Maybe you have something you don't want them to find, such as a journal or candy. Sometimes, you may want to be alone to think about something or because you feel sad. For whatever reason, you're hoping for privacy.

Privacy means being apart from others so they can't see or hear you. It can also mean being secret. Online privacy means keeping your **information**—such as your address, phone number, and even your name—secret from others.

What's the FTC?

The FTC (Federal Trade Commission) is a part of the government that makes rules to protect people from harmful business practices. Protecting your private information, online and offline, is one of its roles. Anyone who doesn't follow FTC rules can lose their website or even go to jail.

If you want to keep your online information private, you need to learn how and why people might look for your information.

5

Who Wants Your INFORMATION?

Imagine your brother, sister, or friends enter your bedroom without your permission. That's what many companies do to your computer. They want your information so they can figure out how to sell things to you.

Other people are sneaky about getting you to **download** files so they can see into your computer. Once the file is there, they can steal information. For example, they might find your mom's credit card number and use it to buy things.

Every computer user, young or old, needs to be smart about their online privacy to protect their information, their money, and themselves.

🔍 Shopping Online

Before you buy anything online, be sure to have a parent's permission. Look for websites that offer a safe, or secure, connection. For example, if the website's address starts with *https* in the address bar, it's usually secure. There might also be a picture of a tiny lock near the address.

🔒 Secure **https://**

Online Store ✕

Websites that begin with *https* are usually safer than websites that begin with *http*. However, thieves have been able to steal information from secure websites, too.

7

🔍 Use Your Privacy Settings

Some adults have pretended to be kids on websites. With your parents' help, check the privacy settings on your favorite sites. Block people you don't know. By doing this, you can keep the Internet fun for you and your friends, and worry less about strangers.

Privacy settings aren't just for kids. Even adults use them to keep strangers from contacting them.

There are so many people online that you don't know and will never meet. However, on game websites and social networking sites such as Facebook, there are ways to interact with strangers. Some may be kids, just like you. However, you can never really know if people are who they say they are.

Strangers may talk to you about things that they shouldn't. When someone online says something that makes you uncomfortable or wants to meet you in person, tell your parents right away. The Internet is like a Halloween mask that people can hide behind so you can't recognize them.

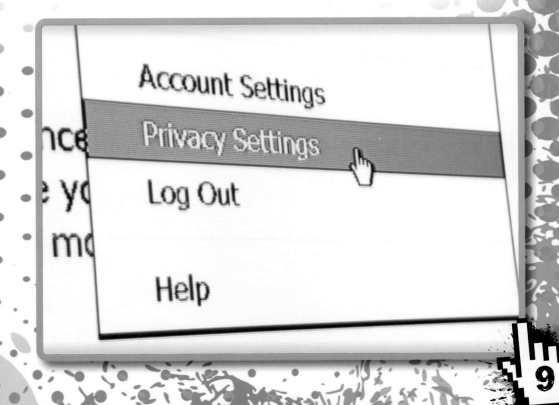

Account Settings

Privacy Settings

Log Out

Help

How to Keep INFORMATION SAFE

When picking a username or password for your e-mail account, choose something that you can remember but would be hard for someone else to figure out. A good password might include your dog's name and other letters, numbers, or characters. For example, if your dog's name is Buster, you could use "Bu$ter12."

Write this information down and put it in a safe place that only your parents know about. Make sure you don't tell other people your password—not even your best friend! Some websites will ask you if you want to save your username or password. It's a better idea to remember them yourself.

Safe passwords are at least eight characters long and include numbers as well as uppercase and lowercase letters. Use a different password for each account. This way, if someone figures out your password, they can only break in to one of your accounts.

Sometimes you need a parent's permission to open an online account legally.

Credit card information is a major target of online thieves.

12

The more information you save on your computer or online, the more things a **hacker** can find. This can be dangerous. For example, imagine your parents let you buy something online using their credit card. If you save the information on your computer, it may allow someone else to use their credit card to buy things.

If you aren't sure if a website is safe, don't type any information until you talk to your parents. Remember, anyone can be online, create a website, or make up an offer. Always check first. Your online privacy—and your parents', too—depends on your smart choices.

🔍 Firewalls

Another way to keep your online privacy safe is to set up a firewall. This is a security program created to keep hackers and **viruses** from getting into your computer through the Internet. It's like a brick wall keeping your computer safe. It doesn't keep everything out, but it does help.

It's hard to think about safety on a game website. Many games let you chat with your friends. It can be exciting to play with new people as well. They can teach you new tricks or challenge you to go further in a game. However, be sure to keep information private when playing, downloading, or chatting during games, too.

When you create your username, try to use something that doesn't reveal anything about yourself. Remember, anyone can play the games you're playing. Even if you know the person you're playing with, don't share any information online that you wouldn't share in person.

Make an Avatar

Use an avatar instead of your own picture while playing games or doing other online activities. It allows you to maintain your online privacy. Avatars are cartoons, computer drawings, or other pictures used to represent you on the Internet. They're a fun way to keep others from seeing who you are.

Don't use your name, age, or where you live when making up a name for a game site. It tells too much about you.

15

Cookies in My COMPUTER?

Cookies are files that help your computer remember information entered on certain websites. This is why your e-mail account seems to store your username. Actually, your Internet **browser** keeps cookies on your computer's **hard drive**.

You can view cookies on your computer to see which websites use cookie files. Some people don't like cookies because they keep track of your online activities. They can help businesses know more about you, too. You can **disable** cookies on your browser, but you may have problems viewing some sites. You can choose to let only certain sites place cookies on your computer. Your parents can help you with this.

🔍 Stuffed with Cookies

Just like eating too many cookies isn't good for you, too many cookies aren't good for your computer. They may make it run slow at times. Be sure to have your parents **delete** cookies every once in a while. Some cookies disappear whenever you leave a website!

s Log-in
sername
Admin
Password
Remember my username
Login

Cookies help your browser remember your log-in information on your favorite websites.

SPYWARE

Cookies remember some bits of private information, but they can be helpful. Spyware programs remember information, too—but without your permission! Companies and people secretly and illegally use spyware to collect personal **data**, such as credit card numbers, e-mail addresses, and passwords.

Spyware is often downloaded along with something else, just like viruses are. Then it sends your information over the Internet to whoever is gathering it. This process can slow down your computer, too. Before downloading anything to your computer, ask your parents. It can be hard to get rid of spyware once it's downloaded.

CARDHOLDER'S REPORT
OF STOLEN CREDIT CARD
authorized to take all steps necessary
se of the above-numbered credit

Too Good to Be True?

There are many websites that allow you to download free games or share music files with friends. Be careful! Spyware may be attached to these things. You may think you're getting something for free, but someone else may be stealing something valuable from you!

...ding File: From: Internet to My Computer

Time left (20 seconds)
...ate 924+ kbs...

Cancel

Every computer should have an antivirus program that checks downloads for viruses and spyware. However, these programs can't catch every harmful program.

19

Online DETECTIVE

Sometimes you might come across websites that exist to steal your information. Always trust your gut. If you have a feeling an offer on a company's site isn't true, it probably isn't. You can also look for clues to spot fake or unsafe sites.

Fake websites often look very similar to the real ones. You might end up on one by clicking on a link. Check the website's address. For example, a website for your favorite TV show might have the name *www.funnyTVshow.com*. The fake site's name may be very close, such as *www.funnyTVshow1.com*. Internet thieves are tricky!

🔍 Not Allowed!

Thanks to the FTC, websites made for people under 13 aren't supposed to ask for personal information unless parents give their permission. If you're on a website made for students and you're asked for personal data, it might be a hint that the website is untrustworthy. And the people who made it may be breaking the law!

20

App Store

2:10

Games

New

What's Hot

Genius

App Store Essentials

SPORTS GAMES

BIG NAME GAMES

nchmark Games

Popular Puzzlers

Even games for smartphones can be used to gather information about you and your Internet habits. Find out as much as you can about a game before downloading it.

21

Gone PHISHING?

When a person or group pretends to be a business to trick you into giving them information, they're "phishing." "Phishing" means using online messages to steal. Look out for e-mails and texts that ask for your passwords, account numbers, or usernames. Honest offers, websites, and e-mails will never ask for those.

Don't be fooled by messages saying your account will be closed or that you won't be allowed on a site. This is just a way to try to make you scared or trick you. Also, keep an eye out for too-good-to-be-true offers. They're often forms of phishing, too.

🔍 Don't Take the Bait!

Phishing **scams** are all over the Internet. Be aware of tricks such as e-mails from people you don't know or who don't address you by your name. Look out for pop-up windows when you're on a site, too. They may have been made by someone phishing for information.

BANK

WE ARE THERE FOR YOU

Online banking is not a sideline to us...it is our main line. Internet trade is not a new way to get additional business...it is our business. You have 24/7 access to your finances. A local branch is as close as the nearest computer. Our tellers and financial counselors are available around the closck to answer your questions. The future is here...

USER NAME

USER I.D.

LOG IN

What can we help you do?

MY MONEY	PAY BILLS
MY CREDIT	OPEN AN ACCOUNT
TRANSFER FUNDS	GET HELP

UNTS

INE
hdrawals
ents

ONLINE

ds

count
Exchange
Portfolio
Status
ch

OMER SERVICE

FOREIGN CURRENCY EXCHANGE

Click here to

VIRTUA

23

acy and Security

Jump to International Banking

Avoiding CYBERBULLYING

Cyberbullying is using the Internet to bother, **threaten**, or scare others. This includes e-mail, instant messages, **blogs**, chat rooms, social networking sites, and game sites. One way to avoid being bullied is to be sure you know the people you talk to online. Don't give your e-mail, phone number, or usernames to anyone you don't know. Using your privacy settings and blocking addresses and accounts when possible can help you avoid bullies, too.

If you feel you're being bullied online, don't respond to nasty messages. Be sure to tell your parents or teacher right away. They can help you decide what to do next.

🔍 Bullying and the Law

Bullying and cyberbullying have become big problems in recent years. Most states and schools have laws and rules about how to handle bullying. The sooner the bullying victim tells an adult, the sooner they can get help. They aren't only helping themselves. They're helping others who may be bullied in the future.

Cyberbullying is just as harmful
and mean as bullying in person.

Think Before YOU SEND

E-mails, instant messages, and texting are all ways we write to people online. Once you send a message, it never really goes away. Yes, you can delete some messages, but many Internet sites save information. Plus, once you send a message, the person on the other end can do whatever they want with it.

Remember that even though you may be talking to a friend, there may be someone else reading the messages with them. People can also break in to other people's e-mail accounts and pretend to be them. Always be respectful in all your online activities.

Safe Searches

Search engines are websites that help us find things online, such as Google and Bing. Keep in mind that some search engines track what you're looking for. It's hard to control this kind of private information. However, you can use certain search engines, such as Ask Kids, that are meant just for your age group.

If you choose to tell a secret to someone online, they can send it to anyone else. Think before you type!

Talking to YOUR PARENTS

Talk to your parents about the things you like to do online. Being secretive isn't safe when it comes to the Internet. Even a good detective can miss clues sometimes. Always make sure your parents know your usernames, passwords, and the websites you visit. This will help them keep you safe and stop people from getting your private information.

What if you share your name or address or do something else unsafe online? Be sure to tell your parents right away in case they have a way to fix it. Remember, information can spread quickly, so be sure to act as soon as possible.

Create usernames and passwords that would be hard to guess.

Use an antivirus program to check your computer for spyware.

Use an avatar instead of your photo.

Don't save personal information on your computer or online.

Keep Your Online Privacy!

Set up a firewall.

Use privacy settings on social networking sites.

Don't respond to e-mails asking for personal information.

Limit cookies on your computer.

GLOSSARY

blog: an online journal. Short for "web log."

browser: a computer program that allows a user to get onto the Internet and look at information

data: information stored in a computer

delete: to remove or erase something that has been entered into a computer

disable: to prevent a system, machine, or tool from working

download: to transfer or copy files from one computer to another, or from the Internet to a computer

hacker: someone who uses computer skills to break in to a computer system

hard drive: the part of a computer that stores all the information it needs to run, including the operating system, programs, and files

information: knowledge or facts

scam: a trick for making money

threaten: to express a wish to harm someone

virus: a computer program that is usually hidden and makes copies of itself that it puts into other programs, causing harm

For More INFORMATION

Books

Jakubiak, David J. *A Smart Kid's Guide to Internet Privacy.* New York, NY: PowerKids Press, 2010.

Rooney, Anne. *Internet Safety.* Mankato, MN: Sea-to-Sea Publications, 2013.

Spivet, Bonnie. *Protecting Your Privacy Online.* New York, NY: PowerKids Press, 2012.

Websites

BrainPop: Online Safety
www.brainpop.com/technology/computersandinternet/onlinesafety/
Watch a movie about online safety and learn more about computers.

Connect Safely: Safety Tips & Advice
www.connectsafely.org/safety-tips-and-advice.html
Find tips for all kinds of Internet activities.

Online Safety Quiz
www.safekids.com/quiz/
Think you know how to stay safe online? Try this quiz!

Publisher's note to educators and parents: Our editors have carefully reviewed these websites to ensure that they are suitable for students. Many websites change frequently, however, and we cannot guarantee that a site's future contents will continue to meet our high standards of quality and educational value. Be advised that students should be closely supervised whenever they access the Internet.

INDEX